E
636.08   7525
Bel
Bellville, Rod

LARGE ANIMAL VETERINARIANS

Large Animal Veterinarians

Large Animal Veterinarians

Rod Bellville & Cheryl Walsh Bellville

Carolrhoda Books, Inc., Minneapolis

for our Katey, who loves animals

The authors would like to express their gratitude for help with this book to Dr. Joe Gessner, Dr. Robert Cleary, and Dr. Foster Soper of the Hoof and Paw Veterinary Clinic Ltd., Menomonie, Wisconsin; Dr. Donna Stevens from Large Animal Clinical Sciences at the University of Minnesota College of Veterinary Medicine; and Dr. Tervola at the South Saint Paul Livestock Market, St. Paul, Minnesota.

LIBRARY OF CONGRESS CATALOGING IN PUBLICATION DATA

Bellville, Rod.
    Large animal veterinarians.

    Summary: Text and photographs describe procedures,
equipment, and special problems faced by veterinarians
who care for large animals such as cows, horses, pigs,
and sheep.
    1. Veterinary medicine — Vocational guidance —
Juvenile literature. 2. Veterinarians — Juvenile
literature. [1. Veterinary medicine — Vocational
guidance. 2. Vocational guidance] I. Bellville, Cheryl
Walsh. II. Title.
SF779.5.B44 1983   636.089   82-19750
ISBN 0-87614-211-0

   3   4   5   6   7   8   9   10   89   88   87   86   85

Veterinarians are animal doctors. They do for animals what medical doctors do for people. A large animal veterinarian treats wildlife, horses, and food-producing animals like dairy cattle, beef cattle, sheep, and pigs.

Large animal veterinarians make house calls. They travel to their patients in trucks and cars equipped with the tools of their trade: syringes and needles for giving injections, bandages, ropes, and other supplies. They also carry their own pharmacy of pills, vaccines, and drugs. Large animal veterinarians are on call 24 hours a day, 7 days a week.

Each morning the veterinarian checks his appointments and plans his stops for the day. During the day he checks in with his office by radio to see if any new calls have come in or if any emergencies have developed that must be tended to right away.

This veterinarian is checking the cow's lungs to find out if there is any fluid in them.

This veterinarian is examining the horse's leg.

Animals can't tell the doctor what's wrong with them or where it hurts. Veterinarians, like doctors of babies and small children, must use their powers of observation to diagnose problems.

This veterinarian is checking to see that the sheep's incision is healing properly.

Maternity care

Emergency care

Large animals receive three kinds of care: maternity care during pregnancy and after birth; emergency care to treat accidents, cuts, broken bones, and sickness; and preventive care that will prevent animals from getting sick.

Veterinarians do a lot of work with dairy cattle. Dairy cows produce huge quantities of milk. To do this they must eat a great deal more than cows are designed to eat by nature, and they must carry the extra weight of the milk. Top cows produce over 100 pounds of milk a day. This is hard work for them, and, like anything working really hard, they will "break down" if something is not just right. These cows represent a dairy farmer's main source of income and a large financial investment. The veterinarian helps protect this investment.

A dairy cow must have a calf before she can produce milk, and a calf every year in order to continue producing milk. The veterinarian above is checking to see if a cow is with calf (pregnant) while the farmer updates his herd records.

This cow has been off her feed. The grain in front of her remains uneaten, indicating that she is not feeling well. The veterinarian takes a sample of her milk and checks it for signs of mastitis (ma-STITE-us). Mastitis is a common problem that develops when bacteria get into the cow's udder, or milk bag. The cow's udder becomes hard, and the milk spoils and cannot get out. Milk from a cow with mastitis must be thrown away. If a cow has mastitis, she will be given an injection of antibiotics (ANT-ih-by-OT-ix).

13

Beef cattle farms are of two general types: cow-calf farms which produce calves, and feed lots where the calves are raised for meat. In cow-calf operations, the veterinarian is concerned with maternity care and calf vaccinations. This cow is having difficulty calving. The farmer and the veterinarian are helping to pull out the calf.

The biggest health problems in feed lots are a result of over feeding and of shipping stress during transportation to and from the farm. Attention is also given to disease control. This veterinarian is taking a blood sample from a cow. The blood test is for a disease called brucellosis (broo-suh-LOW-sus), or "bangs." If the test is positive, the cow will be traced back to the farm it came from, and all of the other cattle on that farm will be checked. Animals that have brucellosis must be slaughtered. This is one way diseases are kept from spreading.

Large animal veterinarians also deal with pigs. They are mainly involved in providing maternity care and care of newborns. Baby pigs are very delicate, so it is important to keep infections away from the farrowing (birthing) area.

Maternity care and preventive care overlap in some cases. These gilts, or female pigs, are being vaccinated for two diseases: one disease causes them to deliver their babies too early (abort), and the other causes death in baby pigs soon after birth.

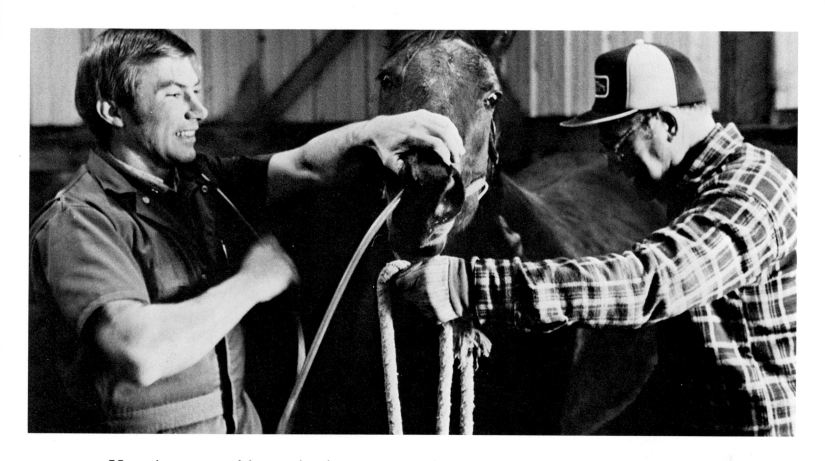

Veterinary problems in horses are determined by how the animal is used—whether it's an athlete, a pet, or a breeding animal. Horse athletes have similar problems to human athletes. Horses that are pets require general health care. Breeding animals need maternity care and attention to any inability to have babies, called infertility (in-fur-TILL-ih-tee).

Horses are especially prone to parasite (PAIR-uh-site) problems. Parasites are bugs like fleas, ticks, and lice that live on the animal, and worms that live inside the animal in its blood, stomach, liver, or heart. Parasites weaken horses by drinking their blood, eating their food, or making holes in their internal organs. It is important to rid horses of parasites regularly.

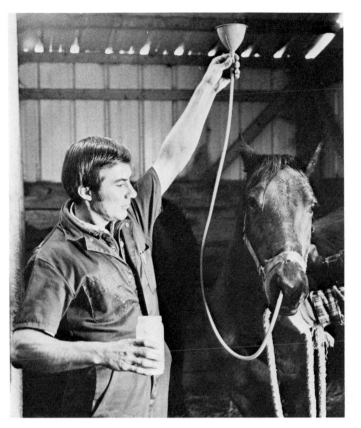

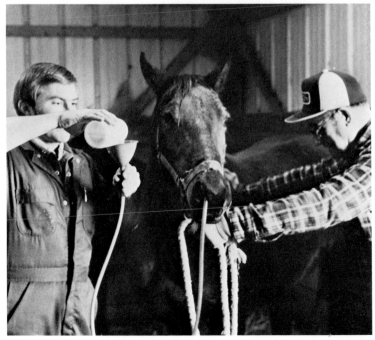

This horse is being wormed. The veterinarian inserts a rubber hose through the horse's nostril and into its stomach. By blowing into the hose the veterinarian can tell if the hose has entered the stomach or if it has entered a lung by mistake. Then the veterinarian pours the medication into the hose and raises the hose so the medicine will run down into the horse's stomach.

19

Parasite and nutritional problems also occur in sheep, but the major problems sheep encounter are connected with lambing, especially with the care of the newborn lambs.

Often when there is a problem with a flock, the veterinarian will check the sheep to determine exactly what the problem is and prescribe a treatment for the farmer to follow.

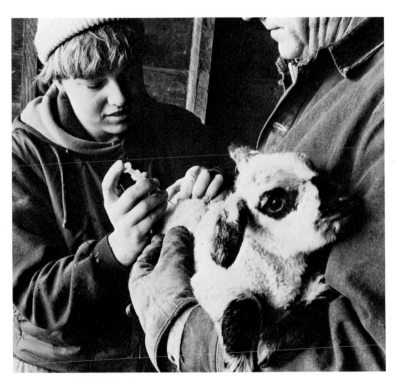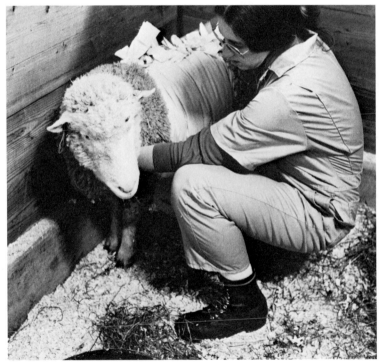

The farmer on the left is giving her new lambs vitamin injections. The ewe (you), or female sheep, on the right is being checked after an operation. The ewe was not able to deliver her lamb, so the veterinarian made an incision, or cut, in her side and took out the lamb.

21

Giving injections to prevent sickness is called immunization (im-yuh-nuh-ZAY-shun). Immunization means protection. The protection, or immunity, comes from a vaccine (vak-SEEN). Many animal vaccines have weak germs in them. The animal's body can protect itself against the weak germs without actually getting the disease and learn to fight these germs if they should ever come into the animal again.

Large animal veterinarians frequently vaccinate (VAK-suh-nate) small animals during a farm visit. The most common vaccination given to small animals is for rabies (RAY-beez). Rabies is a serious disease that is carried by wild animals. It can be given to domestic animals and to people if they are bitten by an animal with rabies.

Zoonosis (zoe-uh-NO-sus) is a term for any disease that is common to both animals and people. Some of these diseases, besides rabies, are brucellosis, tuberculosis, encephalitis (en-sef-uh-LITE-us), and malaria. Large animal veterinarians and medical doctors work together to find ways of preventing the spread of diseases from animals to people.

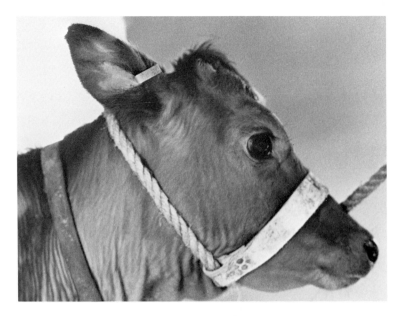

This heifer (HEF-er), or young cow, is being vaccinated against brucellosis. Milk from a cow with brucellosis causes a disease in people called undulent (UN-juh-lunt) fever. The calf's ear is tattooed to show that it has been vaccinated, and black dye is brushed on the tattoo so it will show up better. Finally each vaccinated calf gets a permanent ear tag. The number on the tag is registered with the state. If this heifer is ever sold, the tag will prove that she has been properly vaccinated and that there is no danger of people getting sick from drinking her milk.

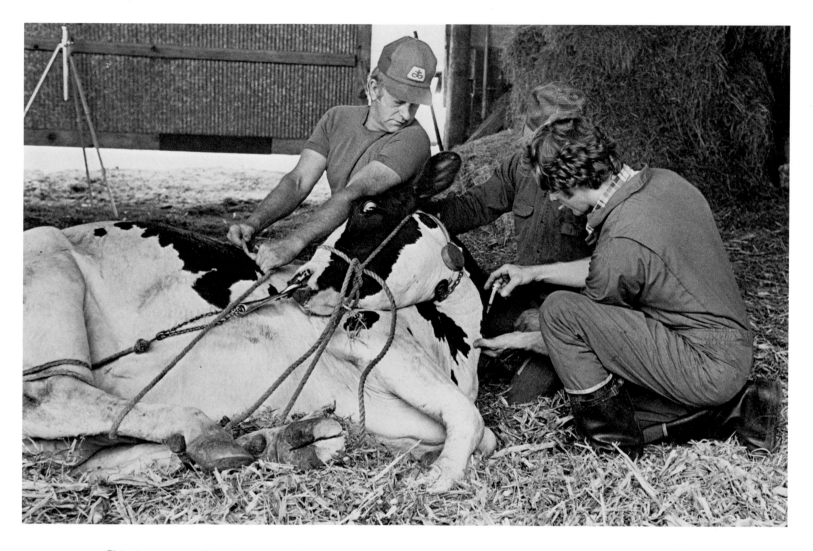

Giving medical attention to large animals is sometimes very difficult. Because the animals are often in pain or frightened, they do not always want to be handled. This cow was lame because of an abscess (AB-ses), or pocket of pus, in her foot. When the veterinarian and the farmers tried to bring her into the shed to work on the infected foot, she threw all three of them into the air and kicked one of the farmers. Veterinarians must be careful not to be injured by their patients!

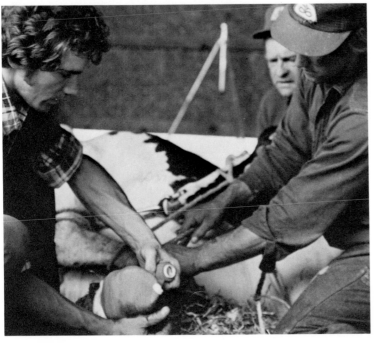

The cow had to be tied down with a rope and given a tranquilizer (TRANG-kwuh-lie-zer) to keep her from struggling. The infected tissue in the hoof was cut away with a special tool, and the wound was packed with a medicated ointment. The cow was then given an antibiotic injection to fight infection, and the foot was cushioned and securely bandaged so she could walk on it comfortably again.

Not all large animal veterinary work is done on the farm. Sometimes treatment needs special equipment that cannot be taken to the farm. Veterinarians have special clinics where they treat animals on an appointment basis.

This horse stepped on something and poked a hole in his foot. The wound was not healing, so the farmer brought the horse to the clinic to be X rayed.

Rocks and dirt were cleaned out of the hoof so they would not show up on the X ray. Then the horse had to be persuaded to put his foot on the X-ray plate.

The portable X-ray unit shoots the X ray right through the horse's foot to the photo-sensitive plate underneath. It takes a picture of the bones inside the horse's foot. After the X ray is developed, the farmer and the veterinarian look at it together. Since the X ray shows nothing in the wound that needs to be removed, the foot should heal by itself if it is kept clean.

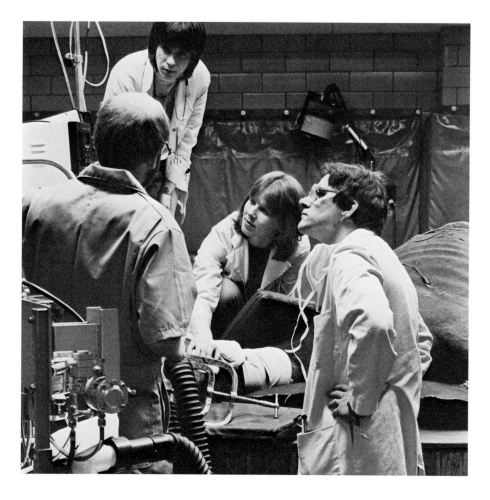

Veterinary students go to veterinary school for at least three years after they have completed college. At veterinary school students learn to use special tools and techniques, and veterinarians research and develop new methods for treating animal health problems. University veterinary schools have facilities to treat large animals in hospital conditions using some of the newest techniques of human medicine. They can provide care which is not yet available in the countryside.

These students are studying a device that monitors, or checks, an animal's heartbeat during surgery.

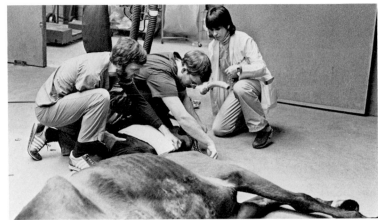
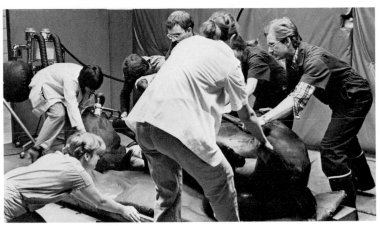
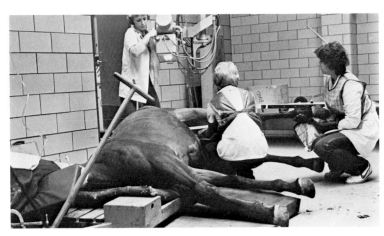

This mare (female horse) is in the hospital for chronic (KRON-ik), or continuing, lameness. She has been given an injection to put her to sleep and must be held up until she becomes drowsy enough to collapse. When the mare is asleep, she is rolled over and a machine called a respirator (RES-puh-rate-er) is used to keep her breathing and to continue administering the anesthetic (an-us-THET-ik). The anesthetic is the drug that put her to sleep.

Then the sore leg is X rayed. The X rays will show if the horse's lameness is caused by bone damage.

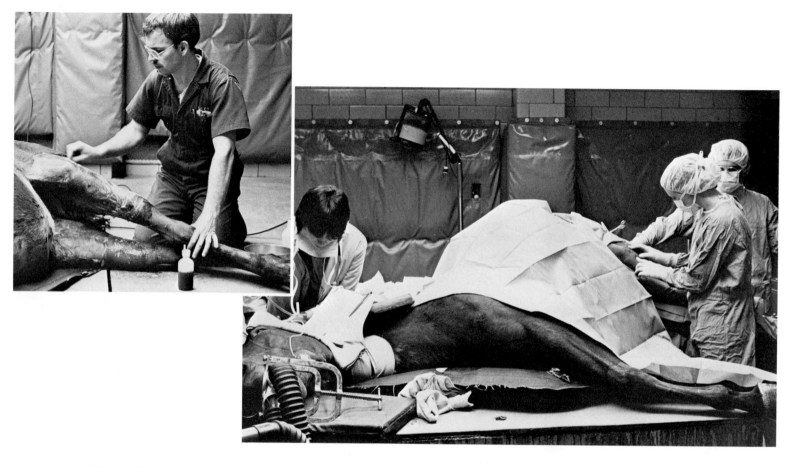

The X rays show that there is no bone damage, so the veterinarian has decided to check other possible causes surgically.

Before surgery the site of the incision is prepped, or prepared. It is shaved, washed, and washed again so it will be sterile—so clean that no germs are left which might get into the incision and cause infection. Then a larger area around the incision area is covered with sterile paper to keep hair and dust from falling into the incision. This is called draping. The drapes are handled with sterile gloves so they stay very clean. When the preparation is completed, the veterinarian checks the location for the incision.

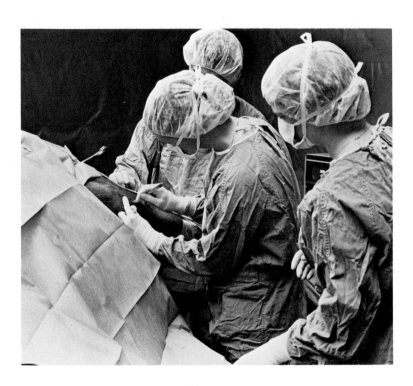 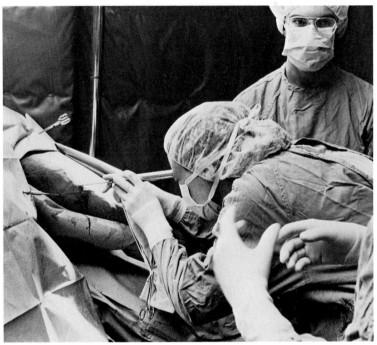

The veterinarian makes a cut and inserts a device called a fiber optic probe in the sore joint. The probe carries a very bright light that enables the veterinarian to see inside the joint. She is looking for any abnormalities (conditions that are not normal), such as torn cartilage, which might be making the leg sore. The veterinarian will then decide if the horse can return to work or should be retired and used for breeding.

Large animal veterinarians make animal breeding and food production more efficient, available, and affordable. They are continually looking for better ways of preventing animal disease and suffering.